MW01101565

Age 6 5 yrs
1st Book

Rising & Falling

poems by

Carolyn Reynolds Miller

Lynx House Press
Spokane, Washington/ Portland, Oregon

Acknowledgments

Colorado Review: Rising and Falling
Cutbank: Forced Marches
Fine Madness: The Girl Who Loved Groceries; The Human Race,
    So Successful at Dying
Hubbub: All Night at the Circus; Lens
Ironwood: Song of the Great Ape
Left Bank: Fugue in Green
The Malahat Review: Coming and Going; The Curved Lens of
    Forgetting; The Last Rites of Love and Disconnection
Poetry Northwest: At Night, New Suburbs, Their Streetlamps Salty;
    At Night, Spirits Come Out of the Trees; Could the Wolf Be
    Presented as a Sympathetic Character?; Fairy Tales on Florida
    Avenue; Ma Bête; Maiden Aunts and the Cello; Mildred and
    the Minotaur; Passing Spectres near Prescott, Washington;
    Surface Tension around the Heart, like Heaven; A Turn to the
    Right, a Little White Light; Walks in Winter

Library of Congress Cataloging -in-Publication Data

Miller, Carolyn R., 1936-
        Rising and Falling: poems / by Carolyn Miller.
        p. cm.
        ISBN 0-89924-108-5 (alk. paper)
                I. Title

        PS3563.I376444 B64 2000
        811'.54--dc21   00-058547

Book and cover design by Joelean Copeland
Cover Art: "Plum Trees," 18 1/4" x 24 3/4" Pastel on card by
Kathleen Cavender

TABLE OF CONTENTS

I

All Night at the Circus / 11

Amazement / 13

Mildred and the Minotaur / 14

A Turn to the Right, a Little White Light / 16

Riffs / 18

Teeth / 20

The Girl Who Loved Groceries / 22

Could the Wolf Be Presented as a
       Sympathetic Character? / 24

The Moon Might Be the White Hole of Calcutta / 26

II

The Human Race, So Successful at Dying / 31

Ma Bête / 32

Walks in Winter / 34

Fairy Tales on Florida Avenue / 37

Rising and Falling / 39

Song of the Great Ape / 41

Praise / 43

III

Emma Indermauer / 49

Maiden Aunts and the Cello / 50

Passing Spectres Near Prescott, Washington / 52

Coming and Going / 54

Furious Basement / 57

Forced Marches / 58

The Curved Lens of Forgetting / 60

Drawbridges / 61

At Night, Spirits Come out of the Trees / 62

IV

Surface Tension around the Heart, like Heaven / 67

The Women He Might Have Loved / 68

Lens / 70

The Last Rites of Love and Disconnection / 72

At Night, New Suburbs, Their Streetlamps Salty / 76

Fugue in Green / 78

Insomniac Circus / 81

This book is dedicated to the women of my childhood:
my mother, Evelyn Hancock, and grandmothers who were
daily in my life —Velma Coyle and Emma Buehler.
And to Bertha Truesdell, who wasn't able to wait for me.

I

ALL NIGHT AT THE CIRCUS

For the hundredth time, the trapeze artist
takes the girl's bare feet in his hands
and murmurs, jump.
She has jumped from so many windows
always just as the firemen
vanish into the net
into the siren. O
  how she envies the gypsy dancer
  collapsed in smoke, shadowy
  firemen jangling in her tambourine.

Down one spotlight blank as a wall
an aerialist is sliding away from his lover.
He wears spiked shoes—proper attire
he thought for scaling a bedroom,
  a girl in sequined slippers
  poised for the muscular swing
  of the elephant's trunk.

Nights of Cabiria. Twenty clowns
scramble out, the saddest hops onto a scooter,
the sky gets lighter, a late customer looks up
to see who has wrung the heart of a stranger.
  Drum roll for the trumpets
  drum roll for the stunt girl,
  hands that smell of sawdust and hemp
  rough-and-tumble under the spell of the lamp.

Almost dawn, and the drummer can't find the tent flap.
Barefoot, the bareback rider invites the lion
into her cage, his paw brushes satin,
his mouth desires feathers, skin
the color of peaches.

Yes, yes, she says, but not now
while the sky is feeding the hungry
apricot petals.

How lonely the cook must be in the kitchen
        the musician prowling
        the lion rehearsing, striking
        the triangle's most poignant
        and unstable note
men and women on hands and knees folding up
canvas and stakes, dismantling
the circus.

Amazement

Inside my head the white rat
looks up bewildered
We've seen this before
between pine trees:
      a cloud-slow barge
              pushing stars

I put the lid on, afraid
      to let the sky move me
a boy and girl on opposite sides of a fire
tending their pulses

So now in the attic
      the old woman stops spinning to stitch
      her face to my shoulder
and crows fly through, stripping feathers
no game for beginners

Sleep is a house of straw
      without water, only miles of beach
         a boy grows old walking

How many are washed up miles inland?
women whose faces blink and tick
      order manhattans
men build shelter
      against the cliff edge, plumed girls
         wade in
            and the crow

       sings as it paces

a good kiss is like a drowning, the ache afterward
can drag the body for miles

MILDRED AND THE MINOTAUR

*—The old embrace each other's silence
like a natural garment.—*

1

A quick nurse limps by, calling each one
by name, lighting little fires
by the side of the road. She calls, *Mildred,*
and two gentle sunfish swim forward.
        Mildred is beautiful
        as a chorus girl
        skittish as a mare's tail,
        straightbacked
        for Heaven tugging
        at her thick white braid.
        Each morning, the angel
        sent to lift her
        turns back, shocked
        by the weight of human hair.

2

In Mildred's room, the Minotaur
has lost his teeth. One horn blown out
the other crumpling, he forgets the puzzle.
When someone wheels forward to ask the urinous draperies
of the wrong bed, "Am I home?", the Minotaur
turns his face away. And Mildred doesn't answer

        either, she's not supposed to
        hover over the shrubbery,
        and the women have let the dolls fall sideways
        in their electric wagons, so she has to dodge
        down stifling corridors to track the prince

deeper and deeper into the cavern
where rocks sing *Stardust* and *Deep Purple*
for the whole kingdom, and the Minotaur cowers
in the wrong room, with an old man's trembling.

3

Tonight the ancients have stood against supper:
they will eat snow.
They have put on white robes for the intermission,
lighter already. The attendants dress them
in heavy coats to hold them down, coaxing,
pushing food, botching the faces of flowers.
But two slip free
shifting their limbs one way and another.
Small leaps shuffle their feet, the walls
open, in darkness they glide and yaw,
and when they tire, the moon pulls them
into its dazzling eye.

A Turn to the Right,
A Little White Light

We imagine them holding on to their ears. Someone took away
the rest of their bodies after we disappointed them, still
they are willing to hear us explain, they want to listen
to our apologies. And heaven stays open all night
for their convenience. Whether

its golden mouth will promise or not, we climb toward the moon
as if heaven were a ladder on top of another ladder
rising from modest stairs. When we look down, the bottom rung
sweeps up to what we hang from, by our hands,

the far side of a cliff above a wilderness
prophets are lost in. The louder I yell
the louder my voice comes back like a heated conversation
until I don't know if it's an echo
or someone else choosing my words: heaven

is what I will never be saved enough to get to.
I can't find that much to confess
and what I find is irresistible.
I might go there under an assumed name

or to paradise on the arm of an ancient
Persian king. I think he's lonely
in that room, or on gold streets where ragged cherubs
fly after the doomed.

Where is the angel of light? People stumble
and death picks them up as if it were piecing a quilt,
shadows on shadows lost to the bone. They want
their familiar face to lie under. How will we know
without clothes, without buttonholes
to hold our carnations? Even tattoos
will slip off with our skin.

Let there be a season when no one rakes,
when all that has ever fallen can drift
with ordinary wings. Mithras, I hear you
out in the open, humming our favorite tune
through a leaf and a comb.
Lead us as if we were righteous
into the blue light of heaven
where no one will forgive anyone
just in case it's condescending,
and we will love each other
to the withered toes.

RIFFS

This beautiful blue is not the sky's
Cellini dredging blue marble
      but radial blue
                measuring earth's curvature
          the fall of iris, like skirts
                draped over buttocks and hips

This blue is not the sky's domestic
          but dawn's three-legged cat
                tossed over blue rooftops
some blue thing dragged down
                a three-point landing dusk maneuvers
          sadness that enters the bone
              blue *you ain't been*

This blue might be the sky's
St. Louie woman
          reedy blues caressing the decoy
                some poor duck caught in a blind
      or a blond ripping free
                from a bindweed bouquet

If I knew which blue I wanted
I'd refuse it:
          a chain of bachelor buttons

          the sky's blue-faced keep
                whose watch runs ahead
                tunneling holes in the cheese
          the last Egyptian, blue-eyed
                his tunic just out of the bluing
          bluebottle, bluefox, blue licks

          a blue onion plate
                of bluepoint oysters

This beautiful blue is not the sky's
rehearsal either
      but a play of blue
          in the round, the world
          detached from its ceiling
      love like oxygen deprivation or
          Stagefright the play I'm cast into

      Which eye to cast in the better part?
          which eye to part with...
and if the *I* offend thee,
          what plucky gestures?

      A clear prompt to cast the eyes down
          without going limpid
to watch god's long blue cigar-ash
grow longer   Curtains
          if you knock it off

Teeth

Dawn
the car with one headlight
I hitchhike awake in the gray interior
            my feet tucked up–Trouble
I can't imagine the driver
       as either a boy or a woman
it's March and my bad tooth is throbbing
       broadcasting pain
through bare trees, rows of men
in brown suits who can't make a Windsor, no color
        except crocus unfolding
               lavender underwear
        So familiar
to be nowhere
pulling away
      or rowing backward
        from something too wonderful to desire
Love without cavities

I'd rather have scurvy than toothache
but when the sailor in the back seat offers
         a cold tangerine
I bite down
      to feel the connection
         only my teeth go off
chalky and brittle, the sky flakes
eerie dashboard green

It all takes place in the landscape
the ache that travels
         migrating kisses, the roadbed's
hardpan layer of bone

In the coffeeshop we sit under separate tables
        reading our fingernails.
Making love is lonely. I talk too much.
My clothes hang so high in the closet
                I can never reach them.

THE GIRL WHO LOVED GROCERIES

When her weight-trainer shouts
    "What ya got—muscle between the ears?"
when the soul food man yells
    she has brains like chitterlings
when a physicist, under pressure,
    makes her dense or vacuous
    according to whim
she admits
    bad luck in men.

If she decides to love a writer from *Field
and Stream*, will she babble whenever
the conversation goes over his head?
If she marries a dentist, will he say
"Your brain, like an unfilled cavity,
rings hollow," or something less formal?
At least he might use novocaine.
Twice a year, he'd give her mouth
his full attention, his hands
cool and gentle, and later,
he'd prescribe something for the pain.

On blind dates, she asks his career
and prepares for the metaphor—
it makes a game of disagreements.
Will a projectionist find her
a dim bulb, back on the last reel?

A girl gets single-
minded: she wants to be right.
Nights, admiring aisles of a grocery
she watches the boy arrange tomatoes, the can man
respectfully bend to the click of her heels.
Tender, how green smocks
stop restocking shelves as she passes,
the box boy lifting a look of esteem.

22

She is dreaming:
they wave from their aprons.
The butcher steps blamelessly
forward, his hands colorful and damp.
He smiles, simply because she rang,
the customer is always
dizzy from hunger.
Barechested to save her shirt,
she's falling all over his big red heart.

Could the Wolf Be Presented as a Sympathetic Character?

*"Then the huntsman drew off the wolf's skin
and went home with it."*— Little Red Cap

Remember the paws. They'll appear later
against red, odd color to walk afraid in
through a dark green forest.

Small for her age, she can balance baskets
of enticement, a one-woman box social.
Many a grandmother's house has been invoked
to pardon a young girl's parade. It's she
who lets slip her destination,
and the wolf, poor devil, nearly the last
of his species, can only slather and curse,
so provoked, surely a human reader
can forgive his concupiscence.

> He waits for her in bed, his lust
> indigestible. Time to think how nubile girls
> wind up old women, better swallow her whole
> and forget the affair in his belly. A knock.
> Her eyes loom big, and bigger.
> > What a nose laid out on the cover!
> > What a sound like dyspepsia!

It's Grandma, already down,
her warning muffled by innards, *beware
shaggy hands on the quilt.*
Too late. He has her first

> and loves her after. One slow eye
> caught fear in the little hussy,
> her sweet curves caressing ·
> his gullet. Damn his appetite!

Tromp and whistle—here's the huntsman
come to fall on his own ax. Little Red Cap
steps out humming, but Grandma, her
small part over, refuses to budge. No one dies
from inner conflict, the wolf lies
sleeping, rock in his gut, a weight
to remind him. Paunch to chin
she sews him up and sends him on,

> he feels like hell. What good
> is a moral now, each path home erased,
> Grandma, her candle years ago
> gone out, the huntsman moonstruck
> in his skin. Strange window, strange
> petticoat a young girl shivers in
> > to watch night rise, full cameo,
> > a wolf's head thrown back.

Hung from nails, her red cloak
darkens like a stain. True
fairy tale, where mystery begins
at the end. Then

> out of the howling moon he'll come,
> moving slower because of the stone.

THE MOON MIGHT BE THE WHITE HOLE OF CALCUTTA

Or Democritus dreaming: when a goddess
with stars on her skirt tripped
on the hem of the known,
atom by atom, he caught his breath,
wondering, what holds the seam?
We answer him quarks and charm, frauds
who have neither heard nor measured
even our own lives, flashes
the moon sends down.

I think we will never understand much, physics
being marvelous, a phoenix.

~~~~~~

Out of our galaxy, in that cool space
at the ringing edge, the alltime greats
loosen up with cricket bats.
Fireballs come spinning from hell,
the batters swing, and the universe
curves back, because nothing
can get past them.

We, in the outfield, fast enough
before the sun comes untrampled
over the snow in December,
see the sky knocked flat, the one
star of winter fall on the devil
and break.

26

~~~~~~

But the parts come together.
Applaud: a woman is rising whole
from the magician's saw. Mended
by a spell? No one suggests love
or library paste, or asks to see the scar.
We admire a good trick, the Minotaur dancing
in the nucleus of her body.
Tight turns.

If the Holy Woolgatherer falls off his spindle,
the world may come ecstatically undone.

~~~~~~

Something's stuck in the fir trees.
Tangents of light glance pink off the mountain,
but in the moon's left eye, a dark bird
keeps ruffling purple feathers. I think

the things of the world are made of
original smithereens, and the moon
of the happy bones of sinners.

> *Guardian star, how far away help is,*
> *sent light years ago, trying to reach us.*
> *On a clear night, when the sky dazzles,*
> *I wonder which is mine, helplessly*
> *tipping his halo.*

II

THE HUMAN RACE, SO SUCCESSFUL AT DYING

Lately, there's a backlog,
so many left standing, shifting
from one leg to another, who can blame them
changing trousers? They want to be well-pressed
among the flowers.

Every spring, the real dead get rambunctious.
They stir things up: one moment, crocus,
then gone, sucked back to bloom
on the other side.

What would comfort the dead?
Only Don Juan does not choose to rise,
he has had enough. But some rough man
who wept in the dark moon of hibernation
wakes from the belly.

Sometimes I am cast down
by a turning season. Then white gulls
fly up, and a blink later, the same
pattern of crows. Beautiful.

In the park, three men are combing the field
for coins. They watch the grass,
and toddlers, whose mothers have brought them
sunward, squirm in their strollers
or run ahead.
And the sky opens, and the plum trees
can barely hold their lures.

Is it for metal
the men are stroking the grass?
With headsets on, they can't hear the tulips,
nor robins clearing their petaled throats.
I think they're dreaming how carelessly
young boys lie down in the fields to rest.

Ma Bête

It must be a spell, so much ugliness
a castle grew up around it, twenty-foot walls.
A curse to rule over: brutes live alone
with terrible faces, and only fresh young hearts
can improve their appearance.

At first he stood in her doorway only in shadow,
or through the garden he let her glimpse his separate path
until she could look without flinching.
So weeks later, when dusk sprang at them,
they stood still as two harts in different sorrows.
In different sorrows, they watched the clouds go cold.
Of course he asked, but she wouldn't.
She bawled for her father.

> Why should he care for her puny skin?
> Hasn't he given her jewels and a magic mirror to play in?
> Instead she spends her day digging among roots in the garden,
> a rodent not fit to be his food.

Every evening, through his roses, she will not marry him.
Vapor from his nostrils envelops her head,
she curves her palm over his gloomy paw and they walk
along the parapet. When she leans into his fur,
when she looks up with quizzy eyes, he wants to be human
with ten harmless fingers. Not allowed to tell the charm,
he makes her dream *The Frog and the Prince.*

> What if she will have him and it isn't true
> about the spell, what if she will, and they go on forever
> waiting for that transformation?
> And what does it matter: she is all bony elbows,
> a hollow at the base of his throat.
> Could he spend a lifetime watching her eat things
> already dead? He won't shed his russet pelt,

handsome as foxskins he rips in his private wood.
And she has taken to calling him *ma Bête*. Is it a joke
to have his face so ugly, to have fur in his mouth?
And he is weary from balancing two legs against his tail.

Every night he sleeps in different directions
so she, stumbling lonely, will not catch him by surprise.
He might take her for a snowrabbit and tear her belly.
Tonight the very room he chooses without reason
she hides in, weeping. He must stop and listen.
It is like the moon's rain falling into his heart.
When he takes hold of the door, he is shocked by grief
in the silver knob. Through his hide
he sees her lying frail as a broken bird,
and naked. She will not know when he enters,
her face a velvet mask
on which she has painted
the face of a beast.

WALKS IN WINTER

1

Near midnight the courtesan walked out
from under cold quilts,
looking up, reflecting the moon
in alternate faces.
      Aging, she carries a mirror in her pocket.
          She remembers
               gathering blue at the edge of water
               peeling irispods to count
               how many rings
               her love would bring her
               white kernels falling
               like perfect teeth.

2

Such is the power of women
where they walk the earth opens
even in winter
small fires spring up in the snowdrifts
twigs burn, hard green
flames appear on the smoketree.

3

The larks are hungry.
Peasant women stroll laughing
under the fir boughs
smoothing their waistcoats
and when they shake their hair and hold up their aprons
fir cones sleek from the rain
bristle and open.

4

Such is the power of women
where they step the earth opens
even in winter
they comb their hair with pine
they rub their mouths with ginger and mint
they taste of pitch.

5

Tonight I skirt the village pond
so long dimwitted with ice
and because the courtesan walks with me
the mud quivers
cold breaks loose from the surface
floating—a great lily pad.

6

I am middle-aged,
almost through bleeding.
My fingers touch the round mirror in my pocket
and the edge bites—
a bit of glass held up in starlight,
one drop of blood like a ruby.
Turned a little
it touches the moon
at the temple
at the throat.

7

Such is the power of women
when they walk together the earth remembers
girls kneeling, sun
on their shoulders. Friends now
we go into the moon's orchard, gathering
starlight, filling our baskets with red
apples and cherries. Such is the power
of old women, they dream
and the earth opens:
they dream the earth.

Fairy Tales on Florida Avenue

Needles stuck in her thumbs,
mouth red from the first sharp bite of apple,
all enchanted, the woman walks
between the spinning wheel and the courtly kiss,
to exercise her only body, corner to corner
reciting the dead cigars:

> *Gretel had a pocket,*
> *Hansel had a bone,*
> *The witch climbed in the oven*
> *And burned alone.*

She met a soldier once who took her
for Pleasure. "Allah!" he cried,
"when a woman dies in voluminous robes
she should float up
like a parachutist in a film run backward,
seven veils stitched tight.
But for any man who has given himself
in battle, the curtains part."

What a racket in the elm:
November counts back its sparrows
lost in April. In plum trees,
rosy shrapnel, a terrible mistake
that seemed to happen years back.
But the sky is clear now,
the lady in the moon is blowing smoke rings
or kisses.

She signaled the merman,
who seemed to know her from somewhere.
When he circled, her arms floated out,
cracks on the sidewalk unreeling
tangled her feet, and wove a net
that began to bear her away.

How beautiful he was, turned
toward disaster. His mouth
found every place free between knots
and bound her in kisses
until a web shone on her skin.

Where is that long-ago-slow rain that fell through her
lovely shipwreck, when night
like a bluelidded dolphin, took the bodies
two by two, and everyone swam ecstatically away?

There is a straight river from here
to anywhere the wind is going.
Seaweed begins to catch around the first strokes
of dawn. And the last bird suddenly cries out
for he can see, far off,
the garden of the mermaid.

Unfinished wing, the wind
is ragged and cold.

If I had a brother, he would love me,
If I had twelve geese, they would all fly home.
And while I dreamed facedown,
They would fold me in whiteness.

Rising and Falling

He is leaning down
to take the gentle bullet
meant for her face,
and the blindfold she carries
always to be ready, strays,
and there—the wounded
under their eyelids.
It is always this way when they talk:
against the wall, waiting for an execution.
Across the room, the safeties go
off and on, out of sync.
One soldier floats to the floor
in lotus position, another is smoking
a fine cigar, the squadron
leader lost in contemplation,
and she, wound tight,
has sprung up seven times for ice.
A fine firing. Uncertain clicks
have made her crazy, so she has shredded
the rope, and now her hands are out,
nervous.

He wants to sit down. There is such a twilight fallen in,
the room gleams and stretches,
a tensed bow. He has built a tepee around her
to catch the arrows. They drift on his skin,
signs of danger: lightning
and a song of moss. He is slipping
on a feather. She calls out
if and *soon.*

The soldiers get up
stripping the branches,
the wind starts shuffling,
the wind is whipping *dance* about her dress,

buds fall like stone
into the moon's meadow. He has told her
to lie down against the wall,
to cover her head.

Beside her,
he is beside himself, weeping. Without orders
the soldiers look away. The soldiers are drowsy
from waiting, so when the order is given
there is a dreamlike effect, the way she reaches,
how he seems to go on
rising and falling.

Song of the Great Ape

So would I rest,
my knuckled paws draped in green shadow,
and watch the blue lake upend
and ibis drift over the surface,
like thoughts that will not come to me.

A season turns over
and over my head, the sky goes deep with pebbles.
There the blackfurred Lord broods, his back farflung
in silver. I sing so he will show his teeth,
and every tree unfolds for Him a thousand buds
beyond my reach. Sleep after sleep,
the round white stone.

I have watched the serpent
walk in his skull and skin. He points, and we are less,
carried off, a dull heap of hair and belly.
We press together, but that lost part remains a hollow
darkness, and we hold ourselves up a little from sprawling,
not to fall in.

When I am called to bury myself in the red pitch
of another, I am the savior tree, sun
beating the grass, I am
He who dwells fullmooned among the lonely,
bruising His chest.
And slowly I forget to climb.
I stroke the moss-backed bark, small as a squirrel
who stops halfway up.

Close under the mother arms,
under the spilling water, the others
have turned their pelts against the river.
But I will open my mouth to look up:

the brightbreasted fruit holds fast,
limbs dip under the talons,
and birds call, *ripe*,
and the tongues of birds blaze
out and in. Oh lovely green
savanna, and the wet vines seeking my mouth.
The wind sings. Twigs rub against one another
until they smoke into blossom
above me, and I would bury my face in their sweetness.
But their bones are frail.

Where is the flower
that can bear my weight?

PRAISE

In lamplight, a woman is bathing
gathering
sheen from nape to hip.
>   The king has worn the rooftop smooth
>   with his watching, as hour by hour
>   endless stairs sink away in the dark.

>   He thought
>   all women beautiful.
>   But the way she let her tattered sleeves loose
>   on the water—this was dawn
>   drowning the ankles of grass.

The trees step higher, clouds wander,
bright moths drowse on their shoulders
and longing blooms from the rose at the core,
which is desire.
>   He swears not to touch her. The morning
>   drought in his belly
>   would strip the desert of stars.

By mid-day, luster
>   pulled loose from the cells
>   in the flesh like dew
>   wants to drip from his fingers.
>   Flowers take on a sharp scent
>   under the leaves' slant green.
If a man bends to kiss a woman
with all the light of his body, if she reaches,
her arms uplifted in gleam,
one river will run through another,
both seaward, light poured out between them.

Twilight. In murderous weather
a woman bathes again before sleeping.
Each time he looks up
      a child throws a handful of opals
      into the desert.
          He sends a servant to fetch her.

He avoids
      talk of war, her husband eight months gone
      into battle. And because she struggles
      like any woman—shamed by her body,
      and because he cannot hold her
      or sing without weeping,
      they tire quickly
      they lie down, damned
      and ecstatic.

Why does the moon scatter its parabolic
light over the human face
and take it back through the eyes
of a lover? No wiser,
they bruise one another.

      Deep under the moon
      mouth of the river
      two seabirds dip to his rowing.
      The male, caught by an oar,
      dies plumed and bloody.
      The female drops in a spiral
      wings flailing—a woman
      above him, her hair gathering
      light on his shoulders.

~~~~~~

Praise the earth that bears us
in darkness among ghost-stems and flowers.
Praise all things five-petalled,
men and women
       trying to sleep in the heat of summer,
       arms and legs outstretched for the fifth petal.
       They feel a spear of light thrust up through the chest
       and cannot explain it.

Praise lovers
       who tend the earth's deep rose, bright
       thorn in the body.

III

Emma Indermauer

Great-grandmother's house trip-trapped
to the cellar. Eight times she danced down

to search among snakes and persimmons.
Eight times she swallowed her children
headfirst like goldfish.
                    And when they were human
she drew them out from the inner edge of her thigh.

Maiden Aunts and the Cello

Afraid to bend, we dance stiffly
each alone, to Mozart.
Who will be chosen?
The one whose dress grows thick
as felt embroidered with Damascus.
Just as she founders, the cellist swoops in
riding a two-edged sword
arm poised like a stem.
The bow leaps upward, points,
whistles straight through her skull
and down her body
as if she were scabbard.
Slit to the groin
her left side is parted
clean away from the right.

      I remember pictures of the female relatives
      faint in summer, ethereal
      and constricted
      and how the blood dripped
      from under the thimbles.
      Girls—seated among pale
      cushions, or in lawn chairs—
           sipping milk
           eating watercress
           sucking the frosting
           from tiny cakes.

The bow moves inside me
at thirteen
a bright light dividing my eyes. I feel
      the nerves sliced, shoulders
      split at the clavicle
      the left ribs marooned from the right
      schizophrenia of the body

I am
the suddenly untouchable.

The cellist looks away while they
stitch me together: chemise, pantaloons,
waistcoat, petticoat, a belt with hooks
to hold up fine lisle stockings
white and tubular
lilies. Cloistered
neck to ankle, shoulder to wrist,

       the maiden aunts sat quiet.
       Smelling of lilacs.
       Always one hand in the lap
       or slitting daisies.
       I am the child breathing
       under the rank wisteria

       under the drawn bow.
With stiffening fingers
the cellist wove me
torque after torque of lovers
down a chain of summer nights
she slid each stem into the tight
opening, and pinned them
in a white-faced circle
around my neck.

Passing Spectres Near Prescott, Washington

"A male silkworm can detect a female seven miles away by odor."
        —Elaine Morgan

That's the way you found us, washed and fragrant,
Sundays when they granted visas. You eased your sweet
black Chevrolets between the posts of drive-in movies
down roads with no streetlights through whatever town
you grew up in, that path itching with summer dust
and stalled lovers.

                    At First and Main
        the same old woman ties things up with string
        and paper, the man who owns the best department store
        has loved one woman all his life, back and forth,
        a scandal at the edge of town, because his wife
        is Catholic, and no one speaks to whores. We wonder
        what *celibate* means, why some preachers aren't,
        and how they get kids.

                    Shifting Detroit gears
I recall every car that drove us on
through adolescence. That year's model can't go faster
than embarrassed idle, or past the thin silk shirt
you gave me one August hot as blazes. Your '41 coupe
hummed like summer. Then you and all the town boys
ran away to wheat.

                    Just over the horizon
        chaff wanders up like yellow ghost ships.
        They carry boys who want to love us, Flying
        Dutchmen sailing John Deere, International Harvester.
        Hot winds blow our love songs over open fields
        miles against the grain, until the tide drops
        and you pick them up like golddust on your boots.

Locked in the bunkhouse, Monday through Saturday,
above a drying wino, did you groan
from your second berth, because they told us
not to touch below the eyes,
and you nearsighted. But we did, behind headstones,
on the mouth, trying not to notice when the moon rose
burning our skin.

      I see you shake against the devil
      rattlesnake grass for dice, your soul
      in the balance: I'm feverish and praying
      Methodist, condemned to save my breath.
      Looking back, I wash in our innocence
      and sail on under summer stars.
      Not one has fallen for how many years,
      old miser in the Milky Way: I want back
      every boy who ever kissed me, seven days a week
      and wouldn't rest on Sunday.

Coming and Going

They have to be fed.
I try to remember
the etiquette: serve
from the right hand,
take away from the left.

Giving Things Up

This time my parents bring me Grandmother's spoon
an uncle's moustache cup, Sandburg's
Life of Lincoln from which the maiden aunts
read aloud in the country dark.

> In the center of Grandfather's great oak table
> his daughter discards a lifetime
> of clothes. I draw out
> a teal blue belt, embarrassed to have taken
> notice, I seat myself in the air
> of grim celebration, at my right hand
> three packages wrapped in tissue: they are
> the pearl handles—knives, forks, spoons
> too thin to hold the silver corrosion. I can't promise
> to want them. But I do
> on sad and formal occasions,
> when my life shrinks
> to a cherished clasp.

Water

My sister lost her voice saying good-bye
to her husband's beautiful faces. The boat rowed
and came back, always thinner,
and when they took away his body

the going echoed—so many dying,
she went to live in the desert. Days of sand
sanguine and purple. She hung her heart
on a violet cliff and commanded *no weeping*.
In the night sky, she counted her children.
And when she had lived like this for a thousand days
a man climbed down
from his stone mountain
on a day without shadow. He conjured
in rising heat a pool of tears
for her to wash in, and began to dance
at the edge, drumming
drumming his feet
until she lifted her face.

An Instant of Grace

All embracing is circular.
The service—Episcopalian
hard on the knees—begins
and ends with singing
we are one body, congregation of luck.
(How many times we looked
away from the nearly fatal
and got away with it—overlooked
the last glance over the shoulder,
the child's hand let go, the wheel
suddenly twisted.)
But some get caught, chosen
years ahead to suffer
the instant.

An uncle's funeral.
The doubters cry and the faithful
keep smiling.

I pray hard
    at the moment of leaving
his spirit felt itself let go,
allowed   to run backward
        to rescue the child
drowned in a backyard pond.

An instant of grace.

Constellations

Which Grandmother said it? At twilight
the birds—done a while with singing—
turn into fish. Except one remains sentinel.
At daybreak, he calls the others
back to their feathers.

Over the Ocean
Stars Forgive Us

My uncle planted his chair
in sweet-smelling grass.
And while he held me, he named them
Orion, the Crab, the Swan, the Dipper.
"Lost children," he whispered,
"are the eyes of Ursa Minor—
one always winking."

        Tonight the angels are near,
        the angels are washing their feet
        in moonlight and sand.

FURIOUS BASEMENT

Sun's up, but let them sleep:
three daughters, the earth
tinder-rooted beneath them.
My father and I are raking up
the pine forest, watching the cabin.
Suddenly we both see it coming
just like Grandpa described it
in a storm, hitting a doorknob
he reached for: ball lightning
barreling down the slope between trees
so fast it doesn't touch dry needles
long enough to ignite them—Smash!
into the cabin. I'm along both walls
yelling for daughters, braids already loosening
into lightning hair. Wives and lovers, I'm shaking
shoulders, telling the women: get out, get out,
and they do, stumbling under armloads of groceries,
lucky not to be fried fish.

My father kneels down by his creel,
and I think my life is over, by now the basement
roaring, and someone I love down there
in a clutch of orange angels
caught red-headed and twirling. I wrench
through into the cellar, test the floor,
stagger through that furious flap
and he takes me, his feet bare—mine too,
on charred cement hot as an iron skillet

our feet are drops of water
dancing.

FORCED MARCHES

Margaret refuses to go a step further.
"This is wrong," she says, suspecting the hall,
the whuush of wheels, the lone
cane tapping. I coax her with passing faces,
the blind woman who never stops moving
   an inch at a time
     tugging the wall rail
       marooned at open doorways
         she rocks her chair, her
           almost weightless body,
             forward, pumping
                the swing until someone
helps her: keep moving or die.
There is nothing to say—
she has counted the last mourner
leaving the funeral.

~~~~~~

One man—genetically cheerful—calls out, beams
and converses. "Winter," he says. Or, "Spring,"
glad to take the place of the turtle, sitting
down to bear the weight on his shoulders.

~~~~~~

The nurse says
Margaret—86 pounds, nearly blind
with cancer—swims every Tuesday.
And the water takes her
gently as a spent camellia,
a foundering wing.

~~~~~~

"We need to go back," says Margaret and remembers
to trust me. We find the room where families wait
to pay a visit. The woman with crayons
has drawn a portrait—bold gestures, stick
arms and legs, a childish body disappearing
inside the head. A kind of petition.

~~~~~~

Going back, we can all walk a little.
Near the door, a Catholic
crosses Christ's chest and forehead—
surely forgiven. When we greet the retired doctor
struck with palsy
or lightning, his quaking arm held up
is erasing unspeakable words.

~~~~~~

God protect us
from the lobby, so many slumped at the wheel, still
believing God will take them.

But no one takes them,
not even into the moonlight, into the circle of angels
who rise, who try to shake the salt from their feathers.

THE CURVED LENS OF FORGETTING

When Mother died, I broke my glasses
and wore her bifocals. They make me dizzy.
She was having trouble inhaling
so they gave her Demerol, which depresses
the breath, I don't understand that.
She struggled for hours, unable to ask

why last summer when Dad's lung collapsed
the doctor accidentally punctured the other
and the machine breathing for him refused to work
and the nurse prepared a huge morphine injection
to stop the moaning–
the sky turned green, the sky turned yellow–

if I don't write this what will connect me?
I've taken everything I can from the summer cabin:
mildew'd wicker, the ice box, the rickety
fireset, Grandmother's treadle with the starflower
drawer pulls, a telephone table from the year
we stopped being primitive.

Each time I go back, Dad's on the roof
in Sunday trousers, with a bundle of shingles.
Mother scolds from the porch step, fingers flaking
Crisco and flour. They're younger than I am.
Room by room, Dad chases until he tags, Mother wheels
inches shorter, arms reaching. They stand
one body, pressed together like hot weather flowers.

Someday they'll reach down and pick me up, saying
who are you?

DRAWBRIDGES

1

Is there a chair rollicking red
under your carpet?
Oh never sit
like straw in a barrel
when apples are riper than maple
the poplar's yellow quack

If I could travel by rickshaw
by hayrick, by tamarack

my parents—newly dead—would wave
atop Pioneer church, from the octagonal
cupola. Around them, gray geese are riding
sidesaddle furniture
and we'd all sit up there before the late great
Abbott and Costello and split our sides

2

Is there a girder, a span
rust-colored linoleum?
Don't wait in a queue to be encumbered
Climb into the sky's lop-
sided blue, magnetic moon
its drive-by monocle
To be uplifted, put on your bib
with the iron buckles

My favorite destination is crossing
long bridges starched and pressed
just as twilight breaks open
sky
in frigate colors so huge
you stop at the edge

At Night, Spirits Come Out of the Trees

What we have called wind in the pines
is that rush of spirits leaving their bodies.
Along city streets, they slip from elms,
the blue spruce riffles, the tree at my shoulder
begins to smoke, a thrill goes through me
in the lavender-scented dusk of an open doorway,
they are on my face, and in the cupboard
disturbing my clothes.
I won't be afraid. If I hold out my hand
they will cradle me all night
in the trough of their even breath,

or take me to a thousand windows,
turning cartwheels, raising dust-sparks
in forgotten roads. They cool the wicked
dream of the righteous. I am with them
whipping the shrouds of the tilting wagons,

I bristle in the savage hair,
and the wraiths move on, shielding lovers
who cannot rise from their perfect pitch.
They carry ecstatic corn silk
to the fingers of young men sleeping,
and touch the ankles of girls
until they wake and cry out, unashamed.

If you were here and I opened my door
for them, they would climb with us
to prepare our bodies in the resinous dark.
Bending, they would clothe us with their delicate shade
and step away, like singing ribs.

Toward morning, a moment of rapture
as they flow back into their branches:
fir trees keenly charged, the hair-raising larch,
the alder in one shudder,
a dogwood seized with joy
to have found its place.
But the last few climb slowly
as golden locusts swarm at the windows,
and suddenly the day has broken
like a red peony, and they can't get back.

And what of the trees left hollow
where small bones sift down among the wandering
children and astonished men?
Oh lonely on the earth,
can you feel them—the empty
that have lost their shadows—how they reach
deep, coaxing the dead to rise?

IV

SURFACE TENSION AROUND THE HEART, LIKE HEAVEN

Stretched new and thin, young men and women lean
against the surface. They don't know what's coming:
a break in tension, the long slide to where we are,
in current going toward the bottom. Silt waits,
lit white with familiar bones.

We trembled so hard the cup fell from our hands
and, swamped in thirst, we dragged each other under.
Spangled chest and thigh, flashing chamber to chamber,
we chose one heart to lie in.
                            We are in deep,
            dropping through each other's dark, past something
            that matters enough to save us, our breath
            a shadow of gill slits cast from the womb.
            You pull strong, you let me swim in your arms.

                    If we could get out
I'd show you a pattern like moiré silk, beauty
that pain bends around stone, all of us sunk here
working the river, broken links in a chain of silver
and our faces shining because of the strain.

            Weapons we take up against the world
            work on each other. Have we evolved from water
            only to sink back like red rock?
                            Over our heads,
            water skippers moor to the surface. Quiet days
            we watch them walk in their halos, moons cast in sixes,
            or six-armed constellations our fins want to reach for.
            Heaven's boatmen. At night, they tap their oars
            on our heart, try to tell us how it's done.

THE WOMEN HE MIGHT HAVE LOVED

                  grow odd
      and beautiful. Their hair gathers in
      twilight, they wait, and when it is dark
      enough their eyes open like flowers.
      I have seen their hands
      mad with repose.

When he asked me what a mirror can see
in a mirror, I told him *desire*,
always over anyone's shoulder. I warned him
the sane accuse us of what we believe in,
then sign their names in anonymous blood.
Therefore, don't tell them
someone has poisoned the grass, that salt
afflicts the left side of your shoulder,
don't tell them the dead come back without a face
or that the drowned cast a purple shade on the water.

Once, he slipped with me over the side of the boat,
we dropped like stone. I showed him
living coral, he showed me white temples
and dancing bones. On the way down, he mouthed
"forgive me for feeding".

      A woman is reciting:
      years later, her husband came back–
      pictures and a bolt of silk–
      and tried to make love to her.
      Her screams, *damn you, damn you*
      drove him away. Hearing,
      the widows collapse.
      Obeying the moon
      the body slows down.

Lucky, he died at his funeral. He didn't hear them
hand back his name like a dropped apology
or see the face they loaned him
wasn't the face that looked out from the glass.

      Tonight the clouds float up thin and tallow,
      the stars chatter like teeth,
      the planets profess their faith in the dark
      socket—they are jewels with their eyes blown out.
      But when I open my mouth, the moon
      tastes of white orchids.

      There is a moth called Tropaea Luna.,
      I name it *Ancient-face-on-a-leaf*,
      I build a tree of bones in a bottle
      and climb in. In moonlight
      I cast my little shade on the water,
      and read the faded names.
      And the ghosts float up, fat on marrow.

I tell them: Pisces.
      Don't touch him or cover
      his beautiful face. Say
      he died exposed, in lieu of drowning.

I believe what he showed me:
      the bloodred card, a photograph called
      Volcano of Rubies.

      In the shell of an oyster,
      the saddest children
      are making pearls.

LENS

1

An old woman said if you weep
directly into the camera
no one will notice. I
have no reason to doubt her.

So if the moon takes off his hairpiece
and lowers his face, rubbing deep
circles, I open the aperture
and black and white dogs
lie down in the picture.

At dusk, I'm walking
out of a habit, out of love
for trees, grass stained darker
than roses that flash and repeat.
The neighbor, tools clanking,
creeps under his car.

2

There are gates across the private
cemetery. In front of a lens
in front of a stained glass window
a pale figure might leap up
and go for the eulogist's throat.
It might be funny except

nothing is sadder—maybe
a child born without crying:
the doctor upends him, swats, mutters
get on with it
and he does, for years and years
until white-haired and feeble, we see him
watering his patch of grass
with the cut open end of a garden hose.

3

We who are about to die
salute you who already did it
in blurred snapshots
your own hands erasing the shadows.

Tonight the moon lowers its oval mouth
into a frame, sighing
O.
A cat wails, a dog
flops at the old man's feet,

the trees pass like ghosts
dipped in lampblack. By moonlight
a man moored alone on his roof begins
the rhythmic nailing of shingles.
I can touch him
without moving the camera.

The Last Rites of Love
And Disconnection

1. High and Dry in the Blue Sand

Three days after the Fourth
I'm sitting on the balcony
watching the neighbor with the crumbling chimney
fly a flag big as his roof
in a big wind, dutiful cloth,
and the ocean, two-thirds patriotic,
unzipping itself, over and over.

I wish there were a rope ladder to climb down
nobody knows where. Where trees
press their bodies close to the grass,
I want to lie in green gone trancey
and when I'm dead, the pine branches
will drop a gentle tattoo *pointiletto*
into my face.

I know my hair could carry a tune
like silver.

2. Other Places to Vacation

Monday through Saturday
the postman finds my body
a perfectly good address.
On his day off, he covers my eyes
with his five-fingered shutters
and whispers, *my little village,*
where will I put you in my foreign pockets?
And though they are not regulation height
nor properly decorated,
he delivers twenty-six letters

which we arrange in droll sentences—
even a j and a bent q jump
over the quick brown fox,
and the dog, who has the postman's number
and the scent of my fingertips
and knows to whom all things shall be forwarded,
circles and barks. In time, all forwarding
shall be done backward, each mistaken
letter lovingly cornered with special issue stamps.
They will not enter Heaven
though I pray for them, because
the Dead Letter Office believed in for years
is dead, our news sealed inside.

3. Getting Off the Ground

Redundant glue, slit
rubber lip of Lepage's,
balsa and tissue, tar for my feather,
I wish I could soar over sand and water,
over the neighbor's American flag
flick, flick, like the swallows,
over the folding family seated in repentant chairs
facing the ocean, over the salt-robed priest rising
on the tiptoes of his best incantation.

4. The Ascension

I wish my heart were on the portico
of a strange city and not pressed in a book,
you, Montgolfier, in your pretty balloon
drifting over my senses,
throwing off a ballast of roses,
and I, Marquise Somebody, nimbly
unhooking all the little sentinels

of my corseted dress, to climb up the rope
ladder—oh, happy floor of your gondola,
to look into cavernous blue and gold
above the Paris exhibit, going higher and higher,
clutching our throats.

5. Thin Air and the Mighty Pen

A boy cursed the rubber lung
of his pen, and a girl hung her head over
the perfectly obscene hoops rolling
off the tips of her fingers, and the boy repeated
by his wretched wrist the wavering tunnels, even
the spiked fence at the risk of impaling himself.
Later, he rarely yells from a postcard.

> Who will free the man Da Vinci caught in a circle
> making an X of himself?
> Beautiful, as all men, as all women
> are beautiful, though reeling with shame.

6. Timing It Right

Once a day, I stand on my head
and the sand runs back. In every house, every hourglass
turns slow cartwheels, until we are drowning
in three-minute eggs.

7. Extreme Unction

Who will know by a casual gesture
the Last Rites of love?
Up and down the beach, the dying
open their eyes. Oh terror
to be Catholic, oh terror
to be otherwise and unforgiven,
waving our flags, closing our zippers,

putting our mail on vacation hold
lest the news, like a deadly flower
finally reach us
years later, when we riffle the pages
looking back.

At Night, New Suburbs, Their StreetLamps Salty

Left behind in glowing sodium vapor
an old tree tries to shake off
poison apples. Belled cows
that coaxed and reassured it
fell one November in a heap of straw,
and the house, its porch cut loose,
was led away in mute distraction
and a hail of purple plums.

Now the countryside is overrun with lights.
Trees no wider than a finger
float in the ground, the garden's slow
ball and socket. The moon tugs,
houses rise like fairy rings
or crocus. On streets named Wildwind Drive
or Saratoga, you want to try out their attics
for walls that won't huff down,
for endless feathers aloft in a ticking.

Lots fit neat as a puzzle
under sky washed out with city glare.
Under triple driveways, gophers
keep butting their heads,
so each house owns its patch of bone and shadow,
its cut of feebleminded stars.

They tell me somewhere people are alive
in meadows. I know what people are
in meadows. I know the wolf at the door
won't always go without a friend,
that someone has to haunt the private rooms

of sticks and glass. In a haunting,
nothing stays in place.
Brooms overwhelm the dreamer
changing umbrellas.

I still think they're beautiful:
streetlamps rare with pink and yellow gases,
carnival lights the way you could dream them,
soft apricot pulp on every corner,
ripe rain.

FUGUE IN GREEN

Every day the furred green worm inside
warming the chrysalis
works out with weights
His last thrust
could light up a forest
    la luna vampira
     sexual on flowers

So spring comes crowbar and bloom
So spring comes tipping the fir trees
turpentine green

      You're growing up the gray doctor said
      his hands leafed out
       twigging her branches
What could she ask
dumbbell, decibel-clumsy

why boys are taller than seaweed
and given to one-handed steering?
why they follow a green noise tires make
      against pavement
why their mouths are thistlegrin
      a girl's two-fingered whistle

Piccolo green, he pulled her down
a kiss for a penny
She heard the copperhead clink

      She wants green smoke, green silk
      a ring if
      the moon had a finger

Ocean floor, mother of green
scattered with shark's teeth
gravity lives where nothing can crush it
neither the wolf eel   nor lord turtle
humped over the murkhole

His touch was fresher than haycock
greener than grapple

Plumb bob, green nail
she in carapace, he in green armor
unfold a house made of hinges
Spring's slow-motion stem
enters the bung-hole

maidenhair, stag fern, applegreen gash
worm in the apple   she remembers
the fig tree
        didn't give a good green damn

———

Dressing, undressing, spring comes dicotyledon
back and forth across fields, lime-green

hypnofixing leafhopper beetles
buzzing clover's green swarm

It enters old men and sends them whacking
They lean on its wickerwood cane
because the world is in meadow

What to do with boyish clamor
a woman's evergreen body?

The moon is shoehorn green!
moonmaple slips at the window, wands

that buckle the knee or make the legs shaky
so lovers lie down for the drummer's green brush

———————

Wrap-around, the skirt had a certain
hollyhock flair that couldn't be hobbled

Even dressed in curmudgeon/crabstick/crosspatch
green would bob October for apples

      This is desire   a crone   prong green
      from the horny toad of submission
      could break her cudgel
      twitching for water
      the smell of green roses

Insomniac Circus

I take down the curtains, a meteor moon
shatters my house like a breakaway window
the hub slithers to find me
notches my shoulder, rides my ribs like a washboard
finds the place where a startled intake of breath
pulls the diaphragm in and up under the heart
(your hand weighing less than a knife blade)

How to perform little acts of sleep
while steering? sad as clowns
climbing out of a
breadbox
the cartoon moves backward:
walls stand up to the fiddle
how now the cow jumps over
    a crescent trapeze
        with a hole in her stomach, (at the county
fair the fifth grade watched
public digestion)

This is what I get for sleeping with the shades up:
    a common
        hole in the chest, and the acrobat
who put his spangled eye to my porthole
springs back reeking of moonlight
his shirt is a bandage

or sawdust
once around, twice around
plum trees ride bareback,
    the ringmaster
        takes a long time unbuttoning his coat